Troubles and Trials Oft Made to Wonder

The Life of Brian Dixon Told in his Own Words

Brian Dixon

Edited by Alan England

Published by Kindle Direct Publishing

1200 12th Ave. South, Ste. 1200. Seattle, WA
98144-2734

ISBN: 9781099501395

Foreword

     I have only known Brian and Edith for a few years. I spent many hours with Brian, having fellowship, talking about the Lord, sharing our experiences of Jesus, reading the Word and praying together. I became aware that his story must not be lost like so many unsung heroes of The Faith; there was so much in it that thrilled me.

     I decided to 'interview' Brian, and make notes. I showed him my efforts after I had typed them up, but such a lot of his life was missed out. Brian then started to write more about his life, filling in the gaps and telling of many more incidents.

In the end, he had written this much fuller account, which both thrilled and inspired me as I typed it up.

I am no portrait painter – I had never attempted one before - but I wanted to paint a picture of Brian and Edith. If you want to see remarkable portrait painting, then Brian's own work is the one to look at.

My painting is full of symbolism. There are references to Brian's love of the Bible – John 3:16 is written in calligraphy. There are references to his craftmanship in making garden furniture, garden ornaments and bird boxes, which he sold in order to send the money to Romanian Christians.

Brian is also talented at painting and sign-writing, as represented by the scroll. The Romanian flag represents Brian's many trips to Romania to encourage and help the

Christians there. The bunches of grapes represent God's fruitfulness in Brian's life.

The flowers, kaffir lilies, represent Edith's wonderful and supportive love, and her love of the garden.

Every Christmas, including the one just gone (December 2018), Brian would dress up in his Santa outfit, and go around to his neighbours' houses, announcing his presence with a handbell. He would knock on their doors, sing to them when they opened the door, and give them a gift of a box of biscuits. He said that he just wanted to spread joy. You certainly did that, Brian!

Brian's greatest joy was to see people coming to Christ, and his preaching was always to this end.

I am sure you will find this story as inspiring and challenging as I have.

Alan England   January 2019

Contents

To Begin at the Beginning

I was born on February 4th 1937, in an end terraced house in Victoria St., Longsight. We moved from there to Marlow St. in 1939. My mother and father were very hard-working parents, and they did all they could to make sure that we were clothed and fed. The Second World War was on the horizon, so these were ominous days. At that time, I had a sister called Iris, who was fourteen months older than me. My brother Bill was born in 1941, and so it was about this time we moved to a bigger house in Earl St.

I well remember the war years, especially the German bombers, and the destruction of the houses opposite St Mary's Hospital, and St Joseph's School on Plymouth Grove in Longsight. I recall the sirens, the air raid shelters and being woken up in the middle of the night and carried by mum to the shelters just outside the house for safety; these were my early childhood memories.

The government had issued ration books, and this meant that there was little food, especially for those with not much money; but we never went short.

Just a hundred yards from where we lived was a park, which the army used for launching the large barrage balloons. Just around the corner, in South St., was a place called Pownalls (Daisy Mill). This is where many of the German prisoners of war were kept. We would see them come in lorry loads, and they would wave to us young kids.

When the war was over there were great celebrations, with parties and bonfires, and the shelters were later demolished.

Dad was a good artist. After the war he painted all the walls in the various rooms with distemper – there was no such thing as emulsion paint – and he painted pictures on the walls in the parlour.

One picture was a copy of Constable's 'Farmyard', whilst on other walls he painted butterflies and various objects. In the main hallway was a picture of a Dutch port, with boats, and our front door was kept open so that people could look in and see the painting.

Mam and Dad did everything they could to make us feel secure.

Dad bought a pony and cart. He borrowed my mam's aunt's garage and made it into a stable. We used to collect all kinds of wood, and chop it up, and put it into bundles. We then went around the nearby houses and sold the firewood so that we could have money to buy food. We also took the pony to Platt Fields Park in Rusholme and gave children a ride for a penny a time.

Dad was agnostic, probably because of the things he saw in the war. He eventually got a job as a mechanic, and Mam worked as a cleaner, with her sister Florrie, in a large Edwardian House in Victoria Park, Rusholme.

Mam made us 'tata-ash' (Lancashire hotpot) for our main meal, especially on a Sunday. It was our favourite meal. If we were lucky, we got 3d a week pocket money (three old pence, about one and a half new pence).

We were encouraged to go to Sunday School. There were a good number of Sunday Schools in the area, and I probably went to them all on different occasions. I stopped going to Sunday School when I was about ten years old. I did not appreciate what they were talking about.

I started school at the age of five, which would be in 1942. I went to St Clements Primary School. I was only there about 12 months, and then was transferred to another school called Ross Place, which was in Ardwick. It was a bigger school, and my sister Iris went to the same school.

As I grew older, I became interested in sports, especially football and cricket. I was the school's goalkeeper. School was exciting. I became a school prefect, which to me was a great honour. My favourite subjects were arithmetic, art and history.

My brother Bill went to a different school in Ardwick, called St Nichols; it was a converted hospital. Bill excelled in sport, especially football and boxing. He was the captain of the school football team. He became the school's boxing champion. He never lost a fight; I was just the opposite, I would run from a fight!

During this time, I did not socialize much; I was a 'home' boy. I tried to look after mum: I did all the housework like cleaning the floors, by using a piece of cloth, with a bar of soap and a scrubbing brush. In those days the floors were covered in what was known as oil cloth. I swept the house and cleaned the trinkets in mum and dad's bedroom. I used to run errands for the neighbours, especially the old folk.

When I left school, at the age of 15, I became a coach painter. I also went to Openshaw Technical College for two years, where I took my City & Guilds exams, and received good marks. During this time, we were taught the basics of signwriting. I took a great interest in signwriting, and I spent many hours practising. In my free time, I used to watch the sign writers at work. I never realised that one day I would teach signwriting at that same college, and that I would one day start the very first full-time signwriting class in the country.

Each week, I would give the whole of my wage packet to my mam. She would then give me back ten shillings for my spends. I learnt to save a lot of my money.

On Saturday evening you would find me at the speedway at Belle Vue, watching the motor bike racing, which I enjoyed immensely.

I was only a teenager when I started to become depressed. It was during this time that my father saw how depressed I was, so he said, "Brian, let's go to the pictures." I cannot ever remember my dad going to the pictures. We went to see Charlie Chaplin in the film 'Limelight'. It did nothing for me – I was disappointed.

Bethshan

My mother also noticed how depressed I was. She said to me, "Brian why don't you go to that place down the road where they make sad people happy?" Why did she say that? I knew where she meant. Apparently, my mother had been there years beforehand, and she saw the difference that God made in people's lives. The place she meant was Bethshan Tabernacle.

Bethshan Tabernacle and My Conversion

I had walked past Bethshan on a number of occasions, but I did not feel inclined to accept any invitations to attend. Religion was not for me. It was for old folk.

One Sunday evening, I decided to have a lonesome walk down the A6 (Stockport Road) until I came to Crowcroft Park. I walked around the park for about an hour when suddenly I felt I heard a voice in my mind saying, "Go outside the park, go to the main gate." I eventually obeyed, and when I arrived, there was a young man who approached me and invited me to a Young People's meeting. This meeting took place after the main service at 8.30pm. He introduced himself as Len Wright.

He told me how he had just finished his army service, and how the other soldiers used to throw their boots at him when he knelt to pray at the side of his bed at night time.   He eventually persuaded me to accept his invitation.

When I arrived, the place was filled with young people. They were singing religious songs. There was a group playing guitars, drums, saxophones and accordions. Every so often one of the young people would stand up at the front and talk about how they were saved. I had no idea what they were talking about. They used words like salvation and grace. but I could not fully understand what it all meant.   Then somebody got up and spoke for about 10 minutes to explain what it all meant. Overall, I enjoyed it.

The people were happy, they had something that I needed. I walked home with a young girl, whose name was Jackie. Before I left her, she asked me if I would like to come to the main service on the following Sunday, and I said, "Yes".

I   remember   arriving   the   next Sunday; it was August 1953. The place was crowded, nearly 1000 people. The service was very lively; they sang a few hymns and then a grey-haired man began to preach. He talked about how we were all sinners, and only Jesus could remove sin, and make us new people. He made it clear that people who received Jesus Christ into their life could be sure they had eternal life. He said Jesus not only died for our sins, but he rose again from the dead so that we could be forgiven and have the assurance of eternal life. He made it clear that if we refused to receive Jesus as our Saviour, we would be doomed to eternal hell.

For years I had been afraid of dying. Every night I used to say the Lord's Prayer underneath my bed sheets. When I finished, I used to say, "But God, don't let me die tonight," even though I was a relatively good person, and known in the area where I lived as a 'Little Angel'.

That night when the preacher gave an invitation to all who would like to give their lives the Lord Jesus, I immediately responded. There were about 20 people who went forward. We went into a small room at the back of the church and I was introduced to a gentleman by the name of Sid Walker. He spoke to me and explained what it meant to give my life to the Lord Jesus, and how I could be sure my sins were forgiven. I remember kneeling and asking Jesus to come into my life, after I had said the Sinners' Prayer.

Mr. Walker gave me a card to sign and to take home with me. It was to remind me of the night I made my decision to follow Jesus. He also gave me a small booklet entitled 'The reason why'. Then he said to me, "Brian, this is just the beginning. You will grow just like a flower and you will blossom."

And it certainly was just the beginning. I fell in love with Jesus. A gentleman by the name of Jim Lowe became my spiritual father, and he encouraged me to become involved in children's work.

The Start of Involvement in Youth Work

The youth work started in an old converted pub. Every Monday evening, I helped with the children. We played games, quizzes and stories. I also helped in the Sunday school. Soon after that, I helped on a Friday evening at another club in Reddish. Tuesday was a youth night, Wednesday was Bible study at Bethshan, Friday was prayer meeting, Saturday night was speedway. I loved speedway until I was invited to a Saturday evening service, and then I soon lost my love of speedway.

Water baptism

At this time, six months after my conversion, I was baptised in water. There were about fifty of us who were baptised that night. It was marvellous!

Open Air work

Beside all this, I became involved in 'open air' work. We held open air meetings on a Sunday before the 6:30pm service and again on Tuesday evenings before the youth meeting. Also, we held open-air meetings at the old bombed site in Deansgate on Saturday morning. This place was full with all kinds of sects: communists, free-thinkers, liberals and evangelicals. It was exciting. We used to go all around the town with an amplifier and preach the gospel to all the people we could find.

We also used to stand outside Manchester City's Maine Road football ground witnessing. Saturday afternoons we did door to door evangelism.

Baptism in the Spirit

Friday night was prayer meeting night. I was going to say a prayer out loud when Mr Parr asked if anyone would like to seek the Baptism in the Spirit. I went forward with some others. Mr Parr laid hands on me, and I suddenly started to speak in tongues. Soon after this, I received the gift of speaking in tongues and someone would interpret. This was about twelve months after my conversion. I still speak in tongues, but in private.

Because of my enthusiasm, my father was a bit angry with me, so he said I must leave home. My mother was upset about this. My spiritual father took me into his house. I stayed there a week, then my father asked me to return. My mother was very happy.

One Sunday night while, we were preaching in the open air, I noticed a young lady who used to walk past the open-air meeting. She was making her way to Bethshan. Sometimes, on Tuesdays, she would come to the youth meeting. At the end of the Sunday evening meeting I chased after her and asked her if she had enjoyed the service. She said, "Yes," so I invited her to the next Tuesday meeting. She came regularly, but I was so busy I never got the opportunity to talk to her again.

I was now about 21 years old; it was 1959.

Edith

About six months later I met her again. Soon after this we started courting. Her name is Edith. I remember one night, it was about 10.30pm, just before we left each other, she said to me, "Brian do you love me?" I was flabbergasted: I couldn't answer her. I had never been asked *that* before! It was not long afterwards that I could say to her, "I love you".

The Lord was very good to us. We learnt to pray and read the Bible together. On Saturday afternoons, after the door-to-door evangelism, we would catch the bus to Manchester and go to the Bible shop, Pickering and Inglis. I would snoop around looking at various books as I wanted to increase my Bible knowledge. I was not a great reader of books but God had put a great hunger in my heart for his Word. I bought the biographies of famous men like C.H. Spurgeon, Moody, C.T. Studd and Oswald J. Smith. Edith was very patient with me! After we finished at the Bible shop, we went to my house for evening tea.

Bible Correspondence Course

It was about this time that Mr Parr, my pastor, encouraged me to do a Bible correspondence course, and I applied to Kenley Bible College in Surrey. The principal at that time was Donald Gee, and the college was owned by the Assemblies of God (A.O.G.). The course studies involved the fundamental doctrines including salvation, justification, sanctification, the baptism in the Holy Ghost and the Second Coming of the Lord Jesus. Other topics included compositions such as 'Why I believe the Bible is the Word of God', 'The value of the soul', and studies in the Epistles, such as finding the key subject and the key word in each chapter.

It was the most valuable time in my young life, for I was searching the Scriptures for myself.

I also learnt much about God the Father, God the Son and God the Holy Spirit: Divinity, Deity and so much more.

I was helped by the assistant pastor, Pastor Barry, who eventually became the principal of the college. I now put aside every Thursday evening in the front parlour from 7.00 pm to 11.00 pm for prayer and study. It was exciting. I learnt what it was to be alone with God.

During this time, I became joint youth leader with a man who had a great passion for young people. His name was Owen Robinson.

I remember Mr. Parr saying to me. **"Brian, I'll make a preacher of you yet".**

Marriage

Edith and I were married on June 2nd, 1962. Mr Parr preached on 'Big Brother is watching over you'. Many of my workmates attended the wedding, and when I was back at work they used to shout, "Brian, Big Brother is watching over you."

Edith and I had our first child April 1st, 1966. We called him Jonathan. He now lives in Australia with his wife Mary, his son Samuel and daughter Jessica.

In 1968 things began to change at Bethshan. Pastor Parr felt it was time for him to retire. The new pastor was George Stormont.

Going to South Africa

Differences between myself and Pastor Stormont caused a strain in our relationship due to the appointment of a new full-time youth worker. He was a good man but I did not seem to fit in with these new plans. When Mr Parr, my former pastor, returned from a tour of America he asked me how I was getting on. I told him I was not very happy. He advised Edith and me to join a scheme called 'Lifelines' that the A.O.G that had started in South Africa. This was a missionary endeavour to reach the Bantu people in the area of Johannesburg. We applied to an emigration organisation known as 'Sameran' (South African Emigration Organisation), and we were accepted. Edith, Jonathan and myself flew out to South Africa in August 1969.

When we arrived, we were taken to a town called Nigel. We were left on our own to sort ourselves out. We were shocked. It felt as if we had been left in The Old Corral: we looked through the window of the hotel and it was like cowboy country, and we expected the cowboys to come around the corner chasing the Indians.

Edith wanted to get the first plane back. Fortunately, we had some friends who lived in Nigel, called Henry and Marion. We found their address, and pushed Jonathan in his pram to Henry and Marion's house, which was about a mile and a half away. They had been there for about twelve months, and they had joined the Lifeline scheme as we had. Marian was a midwife, and she had attended Edith when Jonathan was born. We were so glad to see them.

They were a great encouragement to us. They helped us to become involved with the work. We stayed in the hotel for about a week, and then we were given accommodation for about one month in a house belonging to a mine. The place was called Struisbult.

We then bought our own house through a scheme organized by the council. So, we moved to a small place called Dunnotar.

We travelled about 4 miles each Sunday to attend the A.O.G. in Nigel.

Union Carriage

I started employment at a company called Union Carriage. It was a large company involved in rolling stock. They built locomotives and coaches. They also built what was known as the 'Blue Train', for the Queen when she visited South Africa.

I worked as a coach painter, and also did the sign writing on the main engines. I used to sing gospel songs and hymns while I was working. If I stopped singing, the other workers would shout, "Brian, switch the radio back on"; they seemed to appreciate the singing! Every morning, I would arrive at the works entrance and wait for the buses to arrive, and I would give out gospel literature to all the Bantu boys. These are the indigenous Africans.

There were about a thousand Bantu people who worked there. I used to go to the places where they congregated and talk with them. I picked up a bit of their language. They are lovely people. The white Afrikaans did not like them; "A dead African is the best one" they used to say. Twice I was threatened with a knife by an Afrikaner (white South African). This was because of my involvement with the Bantu.

Every morning Edith would have to get Jonathan up early and ready before the bus arrived outside the house to take him to school. They started school at 8.00am. Jonathan was only four years old at this time. Edith would keep herself busy during the day, and she made many friends. One couple, Elaine and Errol, had four boys. We would visit them regularly; they went to the same church in Nigel.

We were soon in the swing of things, visiting the 'locations' – this was the name given to the places where the Bantu lived. Every Sunday afternoon we would load the car with A4 size gospel tracts and drive to these 'locations'. The tracts were in picture form with a simple gospel message. We would throw the tracts out of the window for the Africans to pick up and read. After we had finished, we would ride around again. It was amazing, there was not one single tract to be found, but you would see them reading the tracts. The tracts offered the Africans the opportunity to write to the headquarters in Nelspruit. We would be informed of the results of those who made enquiries, and each one would be followed up with many showing a desire to follow the Lord Jesus. It was thrilling.

I enjoyed preaching in African churches. The atmosphere was electric; the singing and worship was marvellous. I would preach with the help of an interpreter and you would hear the people shout, "Amen, Brother. Hallelujah!" It really was exciting; the presence of the Lord was real.

Singing

Preaching in the Afrikaners' church was different. It was formal. After six months we moved to another church in a place called Brakpan. The pastor and his wife were ex-missionaries from the Congo. They welcomed us with open arms, and were like a mum and dad to us. Their names were Pastor and Mrs Lees. They invited us to their home on many a Sunday for dinner. One of the first things he asked me was, "Do you sing?" I said, "No, not really. I used to sing when I took some of the young people on crusades each year." "Right", he said, "You are singing this

Sunday." I remember, I chose one of Oswald J. Smith's songs, 'When Jesus comes'. Pastor Lees asked me to preach about once a month plus singing each month. The church was about 80 strong.

When Easter came along, he came to me and said, "You are singing on Good Friday morning at the Easter convention in Johannesburg." I could have fallen over. "Not me", I said. "Yes, you are". I remember I sang, 'When I survey the Wondrous Cross' to a new tune. When the service was, over the pianist came to me and said, "Who taught you to sing?" I have never been taught to sing in my life. "Well", she said, "Your breathing was perfect." I was shocked. There was about a thousand people there.

Pastor Lees made a very interesting comment to me that our doctrinal beliefs were slightly different. He said, "Brian, you are a Parrite, I am a Burtonite." Mr Parr, my previous pastor at Bethshan, believed in conditional security; Mr. Burton (who was a pioneer missionary to the Congo) believed in eternal security. "When you preach, Brian, it comes out clearly what you believe, but don't worry," he said, "You preach how you preach without attacking the way I preach, and I will preach the way I preach without attacking you." He continued, "You will reach people that I cannot reach, and I will reach people that you cannot reach."

In 1970, I received news that my father had died and that the family had already had the funeral. I was devastated; only the Lord could help me at this time. Edith had given birth to a lovely girl whom we called Ruth. I am so glad that my father gave his heart to the Lord before he died.

Visiting the UK

Six months after my dad died, Edith and I decided we would return home to our parents. Edith's dad had already died before we went to South Africa, and when we arrived home, both our mums were delighted to see Jonathan and Ruth. We were so pleased to see them. We stayed with my mum during the three-week period and we visited relatives and friends.

"You're Fired!"

After three weeks we returned to South Africa. I reported back to work and was called into the office. I was told, "You're Fired," (as Lord Sugar would say). I was told that I had not signed the official form before I left for my holiday, but they had never said anything to me about forms before I left. They had just asked me why I was going home, and I said it was because of the death of my father and we wanted to see our mothers. This meant nothing to them.

The real reason was because of my association with 'the black boys'. There were over a thousand Bantu people working there. Surprisingly, losing the job did not seem to bother me. Edith and I prayed about it, and eventually I started my own business doing sign writing. I designed my own leaflets, had them printed, and distributed them to various companies and shops. It was not long before I had sufficient work to get my business going.

I had tried to get a job as a sign writer, but there were no vacancies. In the meantime, I had reported my dismissal from Union Carriage to the South African Union, who took up my case. After six months, I received a letter from the union that I had won my case, and the company had to pay me six months' wages. The Lord was very good to us.

About the same time, I was informed there was a vacancy at a company to which I had previously applied. This was marvellous:

How good is the God we adore:

A faithful, unchanging friend;

His love is as great as His power,

And knows neither measure nor end.

The job was at a place called Springs; the boss was an Afrikaner. He was a lovely man and he helped me improve my standard of work. Within two weeks he had given me a van, and I was doing jobs all over the East Rand (equivalent in size to Cheshire). It was a wide area which included Johannesburg. By this time, Edith had given birth to our third child, whom we called Pearl. We continued working with the Bantu and with the church at Brakpan.

Leaving South Africa and Returning Home

After working with the sign writing company for six months we felt it right to return to the UK.

Willie Smith, who was the boss of the sign writing company, gave me a very good reference.

We were praying that the Lord would give us £800 by the time we reached Southampton. This was because we needed to pay off the debt we had incurred by our visit to come home to see our parents. In order to visit my parents, I had applied for a ticket money loan on a 'fly now pay later' scheme. I had partly paid off this loan using some of the compensation which I received from Union Carriage. We also needed money for our fare home, and the Lord provided every penny.

We sold our home to the council, and sold our car on the morning we were due to sail.

'And my God shall supply all your need according to His riches in glory by Christ Jesus.' Philippians 4 v.19.

By the time we reached Southampton, we had exactly £800 – Praise the Lord! At Southampton, we were met by my brother Bill and his wife Margaret. They drove us home to Manchester.

I learned an important lesson through my experiences in South Africa. I thought I was going to do more work for God, but the Lord showed me that the work He really wanted to do was in *me*. My problem was that I was obsessed with working for Him. This was the beginning of a new adventure.

Return to Bethshan

We returned to Bethshan, and the people received us with great joy. Pastor George Stormont approached me and asked me if I would like to work with him as an assistant, which I was glad to accept. He also approached another young man to do the same. His name was Paul Andrews, and he also accepted the invitation.

I was given the job of visiting the sick and working with the young people. Pastor Stormont gave me a number of magazines to read and told me to base the youth work on the ideas in these magazines. The methods suggested meant I would have to become 'Americanized'. This was not me – I found it very hard.

Controversy

At the same time, an American evangelist came on the scene. He was holding a campaign in Belle Vue. The place was packed; it was a very unusual meeting. The name of the evangelist was Morris Cerullo. Pastor Stormont joined up with him, and this again caused problems for me because Pastor Stormont started to implement the methods of Morris Cerullo in Bethshan. When people came forward for prayer they would fall down backwards, and my job was to hold them when they fell. I had very little problem with people falling, but no one seemed to be healed or baptized in the Holy Ghost. People just said they felt warm heat and fell down, or they saw a bright light. I felt very uneasy: is this God? At the time I could not say whether it was God or not.

Edith and I prayed about it, and asked the Lord to guide us. I searched the Scriptures but could not find it anywhere; most people who fell, fell forward on their faces. According to the Book of Revelation the elders fell down *on their faces* because of the awesome presence of God: 'All the angels stood around the throne and the elders and the four living creatures, fell *on their faces* before the throne and worshipped God.' Revelation 7 v.11. 'And the twenty-four elders who sat before God on their thrones fell *on their faces* and worshipped God.' Revelation 11 v.16.

Peter, James and John, on the Mount of the Transfiguration, heard God speak; 'And when the disciples heard it, they fell *on their faces* and were greatly afraid.' Matthew 17 v.6.

'And when I saw Him, I fell at His feet as dead.' Revelation 1 v.17.

At the arrest of Jesus; 'Jesus said to them, "I am He." And Judas, who betrayed Him, also stood with them. Now when He said to them, "I am He," they drew back and fell to the ground.' John 18 v.5,6.

The suggestion is that only a demon-possessed or rebellious man fell backwards.

I decided to ask advice from some of the top men in the Assemblies of God; they all said, "Brian, stand your ground."

I told Pastor Stormont what I thought, and as a result he brought me before the Bethshan leadership. I was asked to give my reasons why I could not take part in what was happening, but they did not seem very happy with my explanation. George Stormont concluded that I should be dismissed, but the reason he gave was because I was not suitable for youth work.

My dismissal caused some trouble in the church. I went to Pastor Stormont and I shared with him my concern that some people were planning to leave because they did not agree with everything that was happening. I told him I did not want to cause a division in the church.

Droylsden, then Whaley Bridge

I eventually decided to leave the church and went to Droylsden, where the pastor, Phillip Powell, asked me to help him in the ministry. I also helped in the church with such tasks as building and sign writing. My brother Bill, who is very good at building, joined me.

I helped for about two years then I was asked if I would become the pastor of the church in Whaley Bridge. Edith and I felt it right, and I accepted the position. It was a small church with about 30 people. They supplied me with a house and £10.00 a week. To supplement my income, I did some painting and decorating for some of the congregation. I also found private work doing sign writing. Friends from Bethshan would bring us food and goodies.

Edith and the children enjoyed Whaley bridge. There are some lovely walks all around the area, and they especially liked the big park. The Lord was good to us.

Growth of children's work

We started a children's work with numbers of up to 60. We had the help of some younger people who became very enthusiastic at being involved. We managed to use a room belonging to the local Methodist church because of the large numbers.

We also did door-to-door evangelism, and the Lord blessed us with a number of souls who gave their hearts to the Lord, including a family who owned a farm near Macclesfield.

After about 12 months, I was approached and asked if I was interested in teaching at Openshaw Technical College for two and a half days a week. This eventually became a full-time job and led to starting a full-time sign writing class. It was the first full-time class in the country.

Return to Bethshan

I continued on with the pastoral work at Whaley Bridge until I was asked by Pastor Stormont if I would return to Bethshan to take over the youth work. The previous full-time youth worker had left to take up a pastorate in another part of the country. I found that the youth work had gone down in numbers. Pastor Stormont was now in poor health, and had been in hospital. He asked me to do my best to revive the work, and after Edith and I had prayed about this, we felt it was the leading of the Lord.

The Lord blessed us, and numbers in the youth work increased. God was with us.

I was also approached about working at Strangeways Prison to teach calligraphy. Many people will remember the Rev. Noel Proctor. In Strangeways, he had a Bible study class of prisoners in the room above my class. We would hear them singing some of the well-known choruses. This gave me the opportunity to witness to my class. Noel Proctor did a great work at Strangeways Prison. I taught at this prison for about three years; 1978-1981.

Pastor Stormont left Bethshan to join up with Morris Cerullo in America, and so Bethshan went through some changes. First, we had Pastor Rees, then Pastor David Playle.

Confusion

I found myself in a state of confusion. It emerged that one of the pastors thought that my evangelistic ministry was in competition with his, and a threat to his own ministry. He had made these feelings plain in a meeting attended by number of ministers, where he had asked advice from them as to what he should do. I found this very confusing and upsetting, as I thought ministries were to supposed to complement one another.

This particular pastor had one of the best teaching ministries, (using overhead projection,) I had ever seen and heard. Everything came to a head when I preached one Sunday night. I preached on a text in the Book of Kings, 'Young man, give me thine heart'. There were seven people who responded to the invitation, one of them being a young lad who worked for the tax office. That young man is still going on with the Lord today. Bless the Lord!

There were ministers in the service well known in A.O.G. circles. Three of them came to me and complemented me; this was most encouraging. The pastor of Bethshan was not happy and did not like the way things went, and he made it plain to me how he felt. I remember going home, locking myself in the toilet and crying my heart out. I could not believe it. It broke me into pieces and I became very bitter. The

Scripture says, **'Let not the root of bitterness spring up in you.'** Hebrews 12 v.15.

Later on, and with the Lord's help, I was able to forgive this man, and went on to do some private work for him. Matthew 6 v12,14 and 15.

God was using all these difficult circumstances to work in *my heart*.

'Therefore, my beloved, as you have always obeyed, not as in my presence only, but now much more in my absence, work out your own salvation with fear and trembling, for it is God who works *in you* both to will and to do for His good pleasure.' Phil 2 v.12,13.

Joining the Brethren

Edith and I decided to leave Bethshan and join the local Brethren Assembly. We were welcomed with open arms and allowed to break bread with them. We enjoyed great fellowship, especially in the home groups, and I was given many opportunities to preach.

We were with them for three years. Each year we spent time with them on a holiday. We went to Bassenfell in the Lake District, to a large house where we were put into teams. We shared the cooking and cleaning, and went fell-walking. One of the main activities was studying God's word.

It was at one of these camps that our son Jonathan found his life partner, Mary.

Edith was involved in starting a coffee morning on a Saturday, and both Ruth and Pearl helped. A few people volunteered to go to the main A6 road and invite people to drop in. The coffee morning was very successful; it lasted about an hour and a half. We always finished off by singing a few hymns or choruses, then someone would speak for five to ten minutes explaining the gospel.

There was a prayer meeting and Bible study every Tuesday evening. These were good meetings, and everyone was able to share. We studied the Acts of the Apostles, and when we came to Acts chapter 2 then there were fireworks. Dr Shepherd taught us what he believed about the teaching on the gift of tongues, mainly that it ended after the apostles. Obviously, I shared what I believed and what I had also experienced. There was a volcanic eruption. Dr Shepherd, a very gracious man, suddenly exploded. "We cannot have this kind of teaching," he said. His wife walked out. His son Andrew stood up and said, "Dad, do you not realise there are people who have different views to you?"

The meeting closed.

I went home and prayed about it all.

At the next service I went to Dr Shepherd and apologized.

From then on, we decided to agree to differ. Within a few months I was asked to speak on the person and work of the Holy Spirit. Then later on I spoke about the work of the Holy Spirit in the Acts of the Apostles.

Dr Sheppard and I became great friends. We would meet together to pray for an hour on Thursday morning at 7.00 am.

We left the brethren after three good years; it was a time of healing.

I now want to write about my visits to Romania. I will continue the story of my time in Manchester from Chapter 12.

Romania

1991

In 1991, Jo Blackham joined a team that went to Romania as part of an expedition representing Hazel Grove Baptist Church. I did not attend Hazel Grove Baptist Church at that time.

1994

In 1994, I was asked to join a team from Heaton Chapel Christian Church led by a friend called Ian Fellows. Ian used to have a motor factor business in Germany, then he moved to live in Heaton Chapel. The business is now run from offices in Chadkirk, Romiley, by his sons Mark and Andrew.

Ian had set up a company in Petesti, not far from the Dacia Car Company. We travelled to Romania taking with us an ambulance and a car, which we left there for the use of the Romanians. The ambulance was filled with clothes, blankets and medicines which were donated by a doctor friend and chemists. We took a spare car for travelling to various places when we were in Romania, and for our return home.

The team consisted of six people, five men and Ian's wife Myra. I had the privilege of co-driving the ambulance with Ian. It was a new experience driving on the European roads, especially on the autobahns in Germany - driving on the right-hand side in a right-hand British car!

It was a long journey. We stopped in Germany where we stayed for the night in a church, thanks to a friend of Ian's. We were glad of the rest.

From there we travelled to Hungary where we found a small hotel. Ian was fluent in the German language and was able to negotiate a good price for us all. I found Hungary to be a very poor country especially after the political uprising. The shops had very little food.

We decided to have a picnic on the side of the River Danube. We all ordered our food from MacDonald's. I don't know which side of the Danube, whether it was 'Buda' or 'Pest'.

Leaving Hungary, we moved on to Romania. The roads were atrocious. We arrived at a place called Contesti, near Hunedoara.

The church we visited here was an Assemblies of God church, and held about 300 people. It had been built by members of the church, and it was magnificent. The carvings were superb! We were welcomed with open arms, they were so hospitable, and they fed us like kings! The service here was my first experience of being in a Romanian church and preaching.

Whilst here we visited Timisoara, the place of a great political up-rising in which there had been much violence and blood-letting. It was the site of a great emotional upset for me, as I saw the devastation and the bullet holes in the buildings. The young people of the area broke my heart; they were like sheep without a shepherd.

From here we visited the orphanages; what a sight! It was heart breaking. We saw children in their beds and cots, banging their heads against the wall, and I was shocked at the poor state of their bodies. It was horrifying. They had been abandoned by their parents.

From this place we travelled back to Manchester. When I arrived home, it took me two weeks before I could speak about it. I was so shaken and emotionally affected.

2002

This was the beginning of my love affair with Romania. I was worshipping at Bethshan at that time, and I joined a team led by a gentleman called Peter. There were 14 of us, seven males and seven females. He wanted to start a new organization in Romania.

Once in Romania we worked very hard. We provided bags of food which included bread, butter, sugar, flour and oil to give to the elderly people. We read the scriptures to them, gave a short gospel message and prayed with them. We also visited a place called Hobart. Leaving there, we took a cart and two oxen into the Hills of Transylvania; the cart was laden with clothes, food, wood, mattresses and tools.

We stopped halfway through our journey, and called over the people from where we stood. Within no time we had a crowd of people; we sang to them and then gave a gospel message. I was privileged to preach using an interpreter. We then gave them clothes and food, after which they went back to their shacks. We had some lunch and moved further to the top of a mountain. The work really began at the top.

Besides helping more families with food and clothes, we met a 12-year-old girl who had been abandoned by her parents and had been left in charge of two young children and two babies. The clothes they wore were just rags, and had never been washed for a long time.

The ladies in the team set about providing hot water in a tub. First of all, they de-loused the children, then they gave them a bath, and gave them clean clothes. What a transformation! My brother Bill and I set about making a divan bed for the babies. The rest of the lads cleaned the bedroom and painted the walls with white emulsion. This was painted over the top of hardened cow dung! We gave them a meal and food supplies, and then we had to leave them.

We arrived back in Hobart late in the afternoon, then drove back to Codlea, which was about 40 miles away. It was a hard day's work. We praise God for what we were able to do.

2003

I took a team of about 12 people from Hazel Grove Baptist Church and Heaton Chapel Christian Church; male and female. We went by air, and during the flight I had a most wonderful time witnessing to a young woman from Preston. She would have loved to have made a commitment but felt it was too big a price to pay. We prayed for her.

We arrived in Codlea, laden with clothes, which at that time we were able to take as extra luggage, plus the money which I had accumulated by making garden furniture. In Manchester, I had made garden furniture and garden ornaments which I laid out in front of my house to sell them. The sale amounted to about £500, which I took to Romania.

One of the first places we went to was a large hyper-market called Metro; we bought lots of food.

The home we stayed in was quite large. It was rundown, so we did much restoration work, while we were there. Within a few years it was like a mansion. This is where Stephen Potts lived. He had moved to Romania to work among the Romanians and gypsies, and he has done a great work. Stephen was one of the young men at Bethshan when I was involved with the youth work.

All the men slept in one big room on the ground floor, and the ladies slept upstairs.

We had a good team, including a great friend Rodney Bailey, and my brother Bill. They were great workers. We went to the meetings which were electric. The power of God was present so it was easy to preach. Wherever we went it was marvellous. There had been a sense of revival since the end of the uprising in 1989.

As a team, we started out by visiting the elderly people, distributing food and clothes. The ladies were given the opportunity to read the Scriptures. I was able to minister God's word with my friend Rod.

We went to various churches to testify and preach, and visited gypsy camps. What a sight! The huts they lived in were derelict. This is where Bill and Rod fulfilled their ministry, helping to repair their huts, mainly repairing their roofs. We provided them with clothes and food. On one occasion we visited a gypsy church and I remember preaching on, 'The Grace of

God'. There were eight people who committed themselves to follow Christ.

2004

Once again, we found ourselves in Codlea. We took about £600 with us. This time we did not take any clothing as the airline had put a limit on excess baggage, but this did not deter us. We spent as much time as we could rebuilding the house in which we were staying. This belonged to Cornelia and her husband Soren. He was a good mechanic. Rod and Bill set about building a garage for Soren to do his work repairing cars. Cornelia was a very good cook. We spent the rest of the week trying to find time to visit some of the old folk and the gypsies.

Again, we found the meeting was filled with the presence of the Lord. People were being saved. We also prayed for the sick. It was a busy week, with plenty to talk about between ourselves.

2005

Edith and I moved up to Hazel Grove to be nearer to our two families so we could continue to help look after the children. It was becoming too time consuming and tiring travelling three and four times a week from Longsight to Hazel Grove.

2006

Edith and I became involved with the work at Hazel Grove Baptist Church. I had already started working with Mark Paddon, who was then the youth leader at Hazel Grove. I worked with Mark on a Monday night with 'Rock Solid'. This particular year I was approached by the leadership to go to Romania with Mark to a Baptist church in a place called Petesti. This was about 80 miles from Bucharest. When we disembarked from the plane we were picked up by the pastor, Pastor Corneliu.

We were taken to Petesti; a lovely place and a good shopping centre.

Mark and I soon settled in, and we stayed at the home of the elder. We were shown around various places, and we also visited a number of church plants. When we left, we gave them some printing equipment which we bought with money given by Hazel Grove Baptist Church. This church in Romania was one with which we would be heavily involved in over the next few years.

2007

I visited Petesti again, this time with a young man called Jay. He had professed a commitment to the Lord, and wanted to help me. He has now moved to Skelmersdale.

We visited the church plants again; one in particular was on a Sunday morning. The place was called Slobozia, about 40 miles from Petesti. There was a small house in that place owned by an old lady who donated a plot of land, which belonged to the house, in order to build a church. The meeting that Sunday morning was attended by 12 elderly people, men and women. There was no other evangelical church in Slobozia. The area was dominated by the Greek Orthodox Church, which ruled with a rod of iron. They were the 'law'. This little Baptist church was not well liked, but they persevered.

I also visited another church plant in a place called Betesti. I was learning more and more about the Romanians; they were very strict. The pastor took control of everything.

One thing I really enjoyed about Petesti Baptist Church was working with the young people. They loved the Lord and me.

2008

We returned to Petesti with a married couple called Malcolm and Pat. They had been missionaries in Croatia. We travelled from the Bucharest airport on the first motorway in Romania that had now been built. It ran from Bucharest to Petesti, and it was to stretch right across the west side of Romania.

I introduced Malcolm and Pat to Cornelia, and we went about settling in. We stayed in the church where I found they had put in a new bathroom and shower. Malcolm and Pat stayed in one of the Sunday School classrooms and I in another. We had a kitchen downstairs where we made our own breakfast, and at lunch time we dined at the pastor's house.

We had a busy week ahead of us. The first Sunday morning I had the opportunity to preach, and we went to one of the church plants in the evening. Monday, we travelled 40 miles to Slobozia. Here we helped with the building of the new church. It was not all preaching and singing, there was some hard work to be done. For a few days Pat helped with the ladies, cleaning and preparing meals.

During the week I was also involved in painting a sign in the main church at Petesti. It was a scroll with the text, 'We preach Christ and Him crucified'. Wednesday, we went to another church plant, where we took part in the Bible study. The church was packed. I know that Malcolm and Pat enjoyed it.

2009

I went back to Romania to stay with my friends Ian and Myra. Ian had started his motor business. He also had a new house built to establish his business, and I was able to stay with them all week. The business was about 5 miles from the Dacia Car Company. The church was about 10 miles the other way. Ian drove me each morning to the church. Cornel and his wife

Julia drove me around to see various sites. It was a welcome change.

The evenings were spent with the young people. We played table tennis and other activities, plus Bible studies. Wednesdays and Thursdays, we drove to the church plants and helped in Bible studies. On Sunday morning I preached in Slobozia in the new church. I also painted a scroll and a text in this new church, both in the front of the church, behind the pulpit, and the text at the back of the church. It was a good job that I had taken my signwriting brushes.

2010

I returned to Codlea, and I took a group of different age ranges from Hazel Grove Baptist Church. We did the usual visiting of the elderly people. The people from H.G.B.C. were surprised to see the state and condition of the homes, especially of the gypsies at Pasanti. We were able to give them food and we prayed with them. We also went to Holbart, taking two oxen and a cart, laden with clothes and food. We climbed up the Hills of Transylvania, and as usual, had a break half way up. It was exciting as we walked up the mountain singing, "How Great Thou Art" and other songs. We were able to minister to mountain people, and those living at the top. The week soon passed and we were on our way home.

2011

This time, I went on my own. It was an opportunity to go again to some of the churches I had visited in the past. I had some good meetings, and a number of souls gave their hearts to the Lord. Hallelujah!

I visited some elderly people, and went to the gipsy sites. Many of the gypsies would fight in an effort to get food. Soren, who is the husband of Corneilia, took them to one side and threatened that if they did not stop fighting, they would not be given any.

2012

I was unable to go to Romania due to my major operation (28th February).

2013

I went on my own. I enjoyed the company of everyone at Codlea. I visited the elderly people and preached at a number of churches. Sadly, I was reconciled that this might be my last visit to Romania.

2014

This really was to be my last visit. I went to visit Ian and Myra, and I stayed in their home for three days and visited the church at Petesti. Then Ian drove me to

Codlea, where I needed to convalesce for the next three days. It was good, and I am thankful to Ian and Myra, Cornel and Julia, and the church at Petesti. I am also thankful to Steve, Corneilia and Soren for their hospitality.

It has been a great experience. I would still love to go back again, just to see the people. The Lord is good!

A Group of younger and older people.
Their enthusiasm was superb

The sad state of living accommodation

Ready for action.

Building new church (church plant)

Starting the roof of the new church.'

'Moses' climbing. 'Moses Dixon.'

Home for the elderly. Notice the roof.

Preparing the food for the elderly.

Brian doing a sign in the church

Finished sign. 'We preach nothing less than Christ crucified.'

Pastor's wife; a lovely lady.

12-year old girl left with two small children.

Brian preaching at a gypsy church.

Brian preaching at Codlea.

The Coach House

In 1993, Edith and I started to attend Heaton Chapel Christian Church (The Coach House). Again, we became heavily involved in the work, and I was asked to become the leader of evangelism. We did a lot of work in the centre of Stockport, and we reached out to a lot of people. We tried different approaches such as drama and chalk board. We were blessed with a strong group of musicians, and we had great success.

I worked closely with the pastor, Gordon Wright. When I first got saved, it was his brother who had first invited me to Bethshan.

I did some work for the church, including making a 20-foot sign for the outside of the building, painting and sign writing, and I drove a bus for them. This bus was used for bringing folk from a distance, and for Sunday School work.

Church plant in Offerton

Eventually the pastor, Gordon, asked me if I would start a church plant in Offerton. Edith and I prayed about it and decided it was the Lord's will.

It started in a classroom in Dialstone Primary school. We had about a dozen people who came to our very first service. One lady gave her heart to the Lord, and she went on with the Lord until she died.

It was hard work. I was still doing private sign writing work because I was not paid for doing a church plant, and I had to make time for door-to-door work. It was worth it just to see one person come to the meeting and get saved. Others came until we had about 30 people.

We started prayer meetings in our home which were well attended, and we all went to the Bible Study at the Coach House on a Wednesday.

We worked with this church plant for about two years. Problems arose when one of the young men started his own prayer meeting. I had no knowledge that this was happening, and it caused a split in the church.

At this time, I had been diagnosed with prostate cancer; 1997.

The young man, whose name was John, accused me of a number of things, which were proven to be lies, but it was decided in the circumstances, that I should be relieved of the position of leadership in the church plant. The man who caused the problems left to go to North Wales; he backslid.

About two years later, my brother Bill asked me to go to a certain address in Stockport. I had no idea why. When I arrived and knocked on the door a lady answered. I recognized her and she said, "Come in, Brian." As I got into the living room, there stood this man, John. He was pleading with me to forgive him for all the trouble he caused. He got on his knees, crying, "Forgive me, Brian, forgive me." I said, "I forgave you two years ago." I prayed for him there and then; I have only seen him a couple of times since.

Radiotherapy and Child Minding

I was attending Christie Hospital for radiotherapy. Our children were attending Poynton Baptist. Our eldest daughter Ruth married a man called Paul, and my son Jon married a lady called Mary, each couple were married at Poynton Baptist church. We were so happy.

Now, a new chapter started in our lives. We began minding Jon and Mary's first child Samuel, then Ruth and Paul had a little girl they called Claudia. Then Jessica, Jon's baby, arrived after the other two, then Edward, Ruth's baby. Our hands were full!

We travelled from Longsight nearly every day to Poynton, where they both lived. We minded Jon's children because Mary worked at the Pyramid in Stockport for an insurance company. We picked the children up and took them to our home in

Longsight. Mary's mum also shared in the work on other days. Eventually, Jon and Mary moved to Sheffield.

Paul's mum lived in Poynton, so we also shared with her in minding their children.

Jonathan was attending Sheffield University every day on a teacher training course. It was hard work looking after Jonathan's children for two days and then two days looking after Ruth's children.

Jon and Mary attended Poynton Baptist church, as did Ruth and Paul. Ruth and Paul settled in Hazel Grove.

Pearl, our youngest daughter, is a paediatric dietitian. She married Ben, a lecturer at Cliff College in Derbyshire.

Hazel Grove Baptist Church

Edith and I moved to Hazel Grove in 2002. This made it much easier to look after the grandchildren. We attended a couple of churches, and eventually we settled into Hazel Grove Baptist Church.

I became involved with the furniture station working with George Scrivener and Paul Stevenson. George was suddenly taken away from us; the Lord promoted him to Glory.

This left Paul and myself in charge. We worked at restoring old furniture and also assembled pre-packed furniture which we received from John Lewis. This was furniture that the customers returned to the retail shop because they could not put it together. I learnt a lot from working with Paul Stevenson in regard to restoring furniture and woodwork.

Back to youth work

I also began helping Mark Paddon with the youth work on a Monday evening. This was something I loved very dearly. I had been involved with young people most of my life, especially at Bethshan and Central Manchester College.

Mark was a great guy to work with. For a number of years, we went to a youth festival in Stafford, called 'Soul Survivor'. We saw God work in wonderful ways with the young people; it was my privilege to be involved for ten years, and to see God working in the lives of many young people.

It was also my privilege to work with Tim for two years whilst he settled in. Tim is a great youth worker.

I retired from youth work at the age of 78. I really thank the Lord for what He did.

During the time I worked with Mark, I felt the time had come to finish working at the furniture station. After my involvement with the furniture station ended, I was asked if I would like to join the luncheon club, working with older people. Edith and I helped to serve the lunches. I was also asked to give a three-minute gospel message. This I especially loved. Philip and Barbara Clark were most encouraging.

About ten years ago I started a prayer meeting on a Saturday morning, 8.00am to 9.00 am. We averaged about 12 to 16 people every week. The people are very faithful and passionate about prayer. For reasons of ill health, I asked Derek Lindley to take over the leadership, and I thank him for the gracious way in which he responded to. I still attend each Saturday.

Cancer

In 2012, I was shocked to find that I had cancer of the oesophagus and stomach. I should have had the operation at Stepping Hill Hospital, but because there was no bed available, they rushed me to the Manchester Royal Infirmary. The doctor, (Dr Patterson), said to me, "Mr. Dixon, you may not survive this operation, you have a 50-50 chance." I said, "Get on with it, I have got 200 people praying for me: don't worry." The operation took about eight hours.

When they put me in the recovery room, I woke up and began singing and praising the Lord. When Edith and my daughter Ruth arrived to see me, they were very surprised. My daughter had said to her mother, "Don't expect dad to be awake, he will still be asleep." What a shock they had when they found me singing and praising the Lord!

After the operation the doctor said, "I will give you two years." Another said five years. That was February 2012.

It was a great surprise to me that whilst lying in my hospital bed my son Jonathan suddenly came into the ward. He had flown over from Australia to see me. He looked after his mum whilst I was in hospital. Thank you, Jonathan.

My two daughters Ruth and Pearl have been marvellous during these subsequent years.

I thank God for Edith. I love her to bits; she has been so patient in looking after me.

Conclusion

Since my operation, we have enjoyed been involved in visiting some of the old folk on a regular timetable. I am indebted to my friend Alan England who comes to our house, and we spend time together talking about the Lord and His Word. We always spend a short time in prayer before he leaves.

I am thankful for Billy's ministry and for the opportunity to minister on the occasional Sunday morning and evening service.

I value the friendship of Mark and the opportunity I had to work with him on a Monday night in 'Rock Solid'.

Pearl is at the present time studying for her PhD. She is 46, Ruth is 48, Jonathan is 51.

I thank the Lord for his goodness and faithfulness over the past 66 years since I was saved.

'The Lord is Good!'

'Tiger' Dixon by Clair Connor

A Few Things I have Learnt in My Life

1. Don't have too many irons in the fire. The Lord tried to teach me this when I went to South Africa. I thought I was going to be God's Billy Graham. The Lord said to me, "Brian, during the past few years you have been working for Me. Now it is time for Me to work in you." I had been too busy for God to do His work in me: **'For we are His workmanship, created in Christ Jesus for good works, which God prepared beforehand that we should walk in them.'** Ephesians 2 v.10. The Lord had to take me all the way to South Africa to slow me down, and speak clearly to me.

2. When people hurt you and say all kinds of spiteful things about you, forgive them, pray for them, allow God to work in *your* life. In Genesis 50 v.20, Joseph said to his brothers, **"You meant it for evil against me, but God meant it for good..."** 'For it is God who works in you both to will and to do for His good pleasure.' Philippians 2 v.13. 'And we know that all things work together for good, to those who love God, and are called according to his purpose.' Romans 8 v.28.

3. Live one day at a time. The old hymn says, "Run not before Him what e'er betide..." Don't get ahead of God in your plans.

4. "Obey every spiritual impulse that glorifies God." This advice was given me by a godly missionary whom I knew personally. When God prompts you, "Speak to that soul about Me", then obey that voice – we never know what effect it will have. Visit people whom God puts on your heart. Give when the Lord clearly tells you to; 'God is no man's debtor.'

5. Learn to forgive, whether it is your fault or the other person's. I had to learn, **'Be angry and do not sin; do not let the sun go down on your wrath.'** Ephesians 4 v26.**'And be kind to one another, tender-hearted, forgiving one another, even as God forgave you.'** Ephesians 4 v32.

6. Remember God is the God of the wilderness – when you feel alone, and when you don't know which way to turn. He is also the God of the desert, a place of emptiness, but *He* is there.

Now read 'Footprints in the sand.'

Footprints in the sand

One night I dreamed a dream;

As I was walking along the beach with my Lord,

Across the sky flashed scenes from my life.

For each scene, I noticed two sets of footprints in the sand,

One belonging to me and one to my Lord.

After the last scene of my life flashed before me,

I looked back at the footprints in the sand.

I noticed that at many times along the path of my life,

Especially at the very lowest and saddest times,

There was only one set of footprints.

This really troubled me, so I asked the Lord about it.

"Lord, you said once I decided to follow you,

You'd walk with me all the way.

But I noticed that during the saddest and most troublesome times of   my life,

There was only one set of footprints.

I don't understand why, when I needed You the most,

You would leave me."

He whispered, "My precious child, I love you and will never leave you,

Never, ever during your trials and testings.

When you saw only one set of footprints,

It was then that I carried you."

Printed in Poland
by Amazon Fulfillment
Poland Sp. z o.o., Wrocław